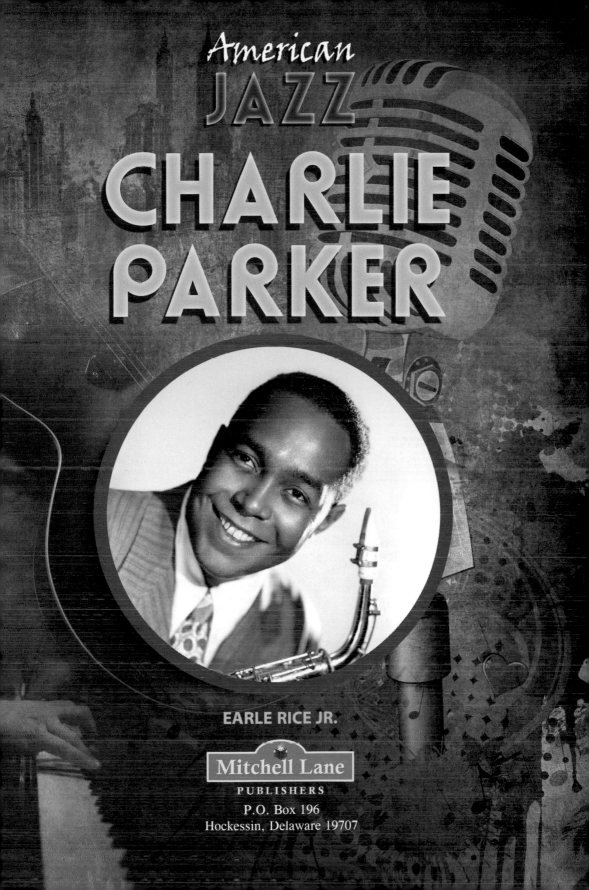

American

JAZZ

CHARLIE
PARKER

EARLE RICE JR.

Mitchell Lane
PUBLISHERS
P.O. Box 196
Hockessin, Delaware 19707

American JAZZ

Benny Goodman

Bessie Smith

Billie Holiday

Charlie Parker

Count Basie

Dizzy Gillespie

Louis Armstrong

Miles Davis

Ornette Coleman

Scott Joplin

PUBLISHER'S NOTE: The facts on which this book is based have been thoroughly researched. Documentation of such research can be found on page 44. While every possible effort has been made to ensure accuracy, the publisher will not assume liability for damages caused by inaccuracies in the data, and makes no warranty on the accuracy of the information contained herein.

Printing   1   2   3   4   5   6   7   8   9

**Library of Congress
Cataloging-in-Publication Data**

Rice, Earle.
  Charlie Parker / by Earle Rice Jr.
    p. cm. — (American jazz)
  Includes bibliographical references and index.
  ISBN 978-1-61228-266-4 (library bound)
  1. Parker, Charlie, 1920-1955—Juvenile literature. 2. Jazz musicians—United States—Biography—Juvenile literature. 3. African American musicians—Biography—Juvenile literature. I. Title.
  ML3930.P24R53 2012
  788.7'3165092—dc23
  [B]
                                    2012008628

eBook ISBN: 9781612283425

PLB

Contents

Changing Directions

Charlie Parker once spoke of friendship with jazz writer and promoter Robert Reisner. "Bobby," he said, "bread is your only friend."[1] *Bread,* in the hip jargon of the jazzman, means "money." On this Wednesday in March 1955, Parker had good cause to affirm his pronouncement. He was down and out in New York City, virtually without two nickels to rub together. This was not the first time fate had found the legendary saxophonist back on his heels and friendless. He would somehow survive this temporary inconvenience of empty pockets and a wallet unencumbered by currency. Of this, he was certain.

On this day—the 9th actually—Parker was looking forward to a weekend gig in the famous Storyville nightclub in Boston. Something always turned up when he needed it most. He had loaded his horn and luggage in his automobile and was now heading out of the East Village—Boston bound. For some reason, still unknown, he decided on the spur of the moment to swing by the Stanhope Hotel on Fifth Avenue to visit Baroness Pannonica de Koenigswarter.

The wealthy baroness was the sister of Lord Rothschild and a jazz enthusiast. Over the years, she had befriended many jazz musicians. Nica, as they called her, shunned the racial conventions of her time. Irrespective of skin color, she routinely entertained jazzmen and other Bohemian friends in her apartment. Her hospitality often raised the ire of the hotel management. This evening, Charlie Parker, rumpled and

The Baroness Pannonica Rothschild de Koenigswarter was cultured and intellectual but was also known for her simplicity and directness of manner. She often presided over jazz sessions for jazz musicians in her New York City apartment, preparing highballs herself and ordering catered dinners.

not feeling well, ignored the icy stare of the hotel desk clerk. He trudged resolutely across the lobby to the elevator. On the upper floor, the baroness greeted him in an atmosphere of Oriental rugs, fine furniture, and soft lights—an ambiance of wealth and luxury.

Parker's visit surprised her, not by his unexpected presence, but rather by his ill appearance. Always the dutiful hostess, she offered him a cocktail. He declined. "Nica, I'm on the wagon,"[2] he said. Now the baroness was *really* surprised. She had never known him to refuse a drink. His refusal cast a new light on his sickly appearance. He asked instead for a tall glass of ice water. She brought it, and he quickly drained the glass and winced.

Calling him by his nickname, she said, "Bird, you're in pain."[3]

"It's just my stomach," he said. "The ice water will cool it down."[4] A moment later, he rushed to the bathroom to vomit. He saw blood. Parker had vomited blood in the past, but never as much as now. A wave of dizziness threatened to overwhelm him. He staggered back to the living room and sat down on Nica's luxurious sofa.

"You're ill,"[5] she said, and announced she would summon her doctor.

"No, don't call a doctor," he replied. "I'll be all right in a few minutes."[6] Parker explained that he was on his way to Boston to play a gig for agent George Wien at Storyville. He did not tell her how much he needed the gig to get back on his feet. His reputation for showing up late for engagements—or not showing up at all—had made it hard for him to find work. His career was in freefall. The Storyville gig represented a parachute—the chance to redeem himself.

Unmoved by Parker's admonitions, the baroness called her personal physician anyway. Dr. Robert Freymann, whose office was nearby, arrived ten minutes later. His cursory examination revealed Parker's history of drug use, peptic ulcers, and cirrhosis of the liver. He asked Parker if he drank alcohol. Parker winked at Nica over the doctor's shoulder. "Sometimes, Doc," he said, "I take a little sherry before dinner."[7] Neither Nica nor the doctor found any humor in his attempt at frivolity. Parker finally admitted to consuming a quart a day of hard liquor.

After his preliminary examination, Dr. Freymann said, "I'm going to call an ambulance."[8] He told them that a hospital is the only place that Parker could receive the treatment he needed. But Parker, desperate to reclaim his fading career, felt he must get to Boston. A hospital was the absolute last place Charlie Parker wanted to go.

The storied life of Charlie "the Bird" Parker began in Kansas City, Kansas, on August 29, 1920. He entered the world at about the same time African Americans created the infectious rhythms of the music known as jazz. Jazz is characterized by strong rhythms, much syncopation (shifting beats and accents), and frequent improvisations (impromptu arrangements). Charles Parker Jr. was born to Charles Parker Sr., a traveling entertainer and Pullman chef, and Adelaide "Addie" Bailey Parker, a homemaker.

The Parker family moved across the Kaw River to Kansas City, Missouri, when Charlie was eight or nine. His father's frequent absences from home led to infidelities and alcoholism. Charles Sr. left his family about 1931. He eventually expired suddenly and unexpectedly when a crazed woman stabbed him to death. Addie devoted herself to raising Charlie pretty much as a single parent.

Charlie earned fine grades in elementary school but showed no early signs of any musical talent. When he entered Lincoln High School at age thirteen, he enrolled in the school's band program. His music mentor

Addie Bailey Parker (above) and her son Charlie Parker (left) as a boy. Charlie was a quiet boy and the focus and pride of his mother's life. Addie bought him his first saxophone when he was 13.

assigned him to the baritone horn, an easy instrument to play. But Charlie soon grew bored with the *coop, coop–coop, coop* sounds of the cumbersome horn. At Charlie's urgings, his mother bought him a used alto saxophone for $45. Her purchase would change the direction of her son's future and send him soaring to the heights of musical greatness.

The Saxophone

The saxophone, or sax, is a woodwind musical instrument. Belgian-born instrument-maker Adolphe Sax invented the saxophone in France in the early 1840s. He developed the instrument to provide military bands with a link between higher woodwinds and brasses. Sax received a patent for it on June 28, 1846. He actually held patents on fourteen types of saxophones. They were divided into groups designed for either military or orchestral use.

The saxophone consists of a conical tube of thin metal (usually brass) with a mouthpiece at the narrow end and a bell-shaped opening at the other. It is often plated with silver, gold, or nickel. About twenty-four tone holes of varying sizes are spaced at intervals along the tube and covered by keys operated by small levers. These holes include two very small "speaker" holes to assist playing in the upper register. The keys, or pad cups, contain soft leather pads. When closed, they provide an airtight seal. At rest, some of the keys remain open; others are closed.

The musical range of the saxophone extends from soprano to bass. High-pitched instruments (sopranino and soprano) usually feature a straight design. Low-pitched instruments (alto, tenor, baritone, and bass) would become unacceptably long if straight. Instead, they generally incorporate a U-bend. This bend has become the iconic feature of the saxophone family. To play the instrument, the musician blows on a flat cane reed in the mouthpiece while fingering the keys open or closed to produce the desired tones.

Statue of Adolphe Sax in Dinant, Belgium

Chapter 2

Fast Company

After moving to Missouri, the Parker family lived in a two-story frame house at 1516 Olive Street. Their new home lay in the heart of Kansas City's black ghetto. It stood within easy walking distance of the city's garish entertainment district a few blocks away. Its closeness to the center of the jazz scene in America's heartland would have a profound effect on young Charlie.

Charlie's formative years—from 1928 to 1939—exactly coincided with the era of corrupt Democratic machine government in Kansas City. Under political boss Tom Pendergast, the city underwent a jazz renaissance. It enjoyed a dozen years of good times. Its near-endless array of cabarets, nightclubs, dance halls, show bars, music lounges, speakeasies, honky-tonks, taverns, bars, and saloons provided the finest on-the-job training in the world for jazz musicians. Seasoned musicians found full employment there. Charlie Parker was soon to become one of Kansas City's leading jazz apprentices.

Kansas City was the Las Vegas of its day. Its promise of paying gigs became a magnet for most of the great jazz icons of the 1930s. Musicians of note who appeared there included Count Basie, Mary Lou Williams, Lester Young, Hot Lips Page, Ben Webster, Buster Smith, Herschel Evans, Jay McShann, Bennie Moten, and many more. Nationally famous touring bands also answered the lure of full employment in Kansas City. Among them were those of Duke Ellington, Cab Calloway,

Edward Kennedy "Duke" Ellington (seated) and his orchestra.
Ellington, pianist, band leader, composer, and arranger,
formed his band in 1924 and often appeared in Kansas City
during the early 1930s. Ellington's musicianship influenced
young Charlie Parker and scores of other jazzmen.

Fletcher Henderson, and Jimmy Lunceford. These bands featured such
performers as Coleman Hawkins, Johnny Hodges, Barney Bigard, Willie
Smith, Chu Berry, and Dizzy Gillespie. Charlie would not lack for role
models.

Young Charlie received his first formal musical training under band
director Alonzo Lewis at Lincoln High School. He learned how to read
music and play accurately off a musical score. He soon began practicing
on his alto horn with fellow student Lawrence "88" Keyes, a pianist.
Keyes taught him a lot about harmonics (musical overtones). "If [Charlie]
had been as conscientious about his high school work as he was about
his music," Keyes said later, "he would have become a professor."[1]

Trombonist Robert Simpson also befriended Charlie. In a later
interview, Keyes said that he, Simpson, and Charlie formed a "triumvirate
. . . the three of us would hang out in each other's houses, practicing

and talking music day and night."[2] Those closest to Charlie believe Simpson was probably the best friend he ever had.

Charlie soon began to hang around outside the local nightclubs to listen to the musicians jamming (improvising) inside. He especially admired tenor saxophonist Lester Young. Charlie would finger his own sax along with the sounds of Young's smooth, mellow tones. He dreamed of the day when he could sit in and jam with the likes of Lester, Herschel Evans, and Ben Webster. Charlie practiced fifteen hours a day. He was awakening to his musical potential. At the same time, he was experiencing another kind of awakening.

In April 1934, Addie rented out the upper rooms of the Parker home to the Ruffin family. The family consisted of pretty fourteen-year-old Rebecca Ellen Ruffin, her mother, brother, and four sisters. Charlie

Lester "Prez" Young, a major stylist on the tenor saxophone, joined William "Count" Basie's band in 1936. Known for his gentle tone and ethereal lyricism, his subtle harmonies and unconventional rhythmic independence inspired both bebop and cool-jazz musicians.

slowly became attracted to the dark-haired Rebecca, who looked like a young Lena Horne. She struck a spark inside him that began to smolder.

In 1935, Charlie quit school. At the urging of Robert Simpson, he joined Keyes's band, the Deans of Swing. At the age of fourteen, Charlie gave his age as eighteen and joined the local musician's union. When he got his union card, he began to play regular gigs at the city's Greenleaf Gardens. He earned only $1.25 a night, but he was now a pro.

Not long after his professional debut, Charlie suffered a terrible blow. Robert Simpson died of a heart condition on the operating table at the age of twenty-one. Years later, still scarred by Simpson's death, he kept an acquaintance from drawing too close to him. Asked why, he explained, "Once in Kansas City I had a friend who I liked very much, and a sorrowful thing happened. . . . He died."[3] Some sources think that the loss of his friend may have contributed to Charlie's sudden appetite for benzedrine inhalers, marijuana, and hard liquor. He had lost the support of someone who had truly believed in him.

In the spring of 1936, Charlie hit another speed bump on the road to his maturity. One night at the rowdy Reno Club, drummer Jo Jones organized a jam session at the end of the last set by Count Basie. Nearly every jazzman in the city was in the house. Charlie decided to sit in. Bassist Gene Ramey warned him that he might not be ready yet. "Fast company," he said. "Maybe you'd better sit this one out."[4] Charlie jumped in anyway.

Jo Jones marked time behind Charlie, hitting accents on the high-hat cymbal. Jo's deft strokes on the thin metal produced beautiful sounds. The group was jamming on "I Got Rhythm," which was fine with Charlie. He knew the changes—the interludes within which the musical key changed. His first change went off well. It took him out of key, which was fine, until he realized he did not know how to get back on key.

Charlie faltered, tried to recover, then lost his grip on the time (beat), a cardinal sin for all musicians. Jones stopped drumming and sailed his cymbal at Charlie. It crashed at his feet with a shattering

William "Count" Basie, jazz pianist, composer, and bandleader, formed his band in Kansas City, Missouri, in 1936 and went on to become America's premier representative of swing. His career spanned five decades, featuring such inimitable hits as "One O'Clock Jump" and "April in Paris."

Drummer Jonathan "Jo" Jones rose to fame in jazzdom with Count Basie's orchestra. He was known for his smooth, effortless beat, his perfect touch on the high-hat cymbal, and his unsurpassed ability to play behind soloists such as Charlie Parker.

clatter. A heckler in the audience called out, "Who's next up there?"[5] Charlie had been rudely "gonged" off the stage.

With laughter still ringing in his ears, Charlie left the club. "I'll be back," he said to himself. "I'll fix these cats."[6]

Destination Genius

By any standard, Charlie Parker was a musical phenomenon. He owed his artistic genius in part to his natural talent. But the perfection of his art came from self-determination and dedication—and practice, practice, practice. Arguably, he became the most influential jazz musician of his time. His dominance in the world of jazz continues to this day. Much of what he learned on his way to the heights of jazz musicianship he taught himself. And he did it his way—which is another way of saying the hard way.

"If genius is the capacity for taking infinite pains," observed Ross Russell, one of Charlie's biographers, "it may also be a matter of taking a wrong course and arriving at a new destination."[7] Parker learned early on that there were twelve major keys and scales in music. Armed with this knowledge, he reasoned that he would have to learn to play in all twelve keys.

What Parker did not know was that most jazz is performed in very few keys. Most jazzmen felt uncomfortable in more than three or perhaps four keys. Count Basie, for instance, played everything in B-flat. But no one bothered to tell Parker, and he did not ask anyone. He set himself the task of mastering all twelve keys and scales. Starting with the scale of C, he moved up a half tone and learned the scale of D-flat, then upward through the remaining ten tones (or keys). Taking a wrong course, Charlie Parker arrived at a new destination called genius.

12 Major Scales and Arpeggios for Eb Alto Saxophone

Chapter 3

Ready Now

In the summer of 1936, Charlie Parker told his mother that he planned to marry Rebecca Ruffin. Addie objected. Charlie countered. "Mama, I'm in love," he said. "And I'm old enough to get married."[1] He proposed to Rebecca on July 24. They were married in the Kansas City Courthouse the next day. Their marriage would last for five years.

Later in 1936, Parker was involved in an automobile accident while traveling to a Thanksgiving Day gig in Jefferson City, Missouri. One of his companions was killed, and Parker sustained three broken ribs and a spinal fracture. After Rebecca caught Charlie using a needle, his doctor told Rebecca, "I don't know if you can understand it or not, but Charlie has to take heroin to kill the pain from his ribs and spine."[2]

Parker later became an addict with a huge tolerance for drugs at an early age. In 1941, however, he offered a different reason for his addiction. "It all came from being introduced too early to night life,"[3] he said. In either case, the drug monkey rode his back for the rest of his life.

The following year, Parker spent the summer of 1937 with George E. Lee's band at a resort in Eldon, Missouri, in the Ozarks. Working with pianist and guitarist Carrie Powell, he began experimenting with harmony. (Harmony is a pleasant chord or progression of chords; a chord is a combination of notes sounded together to produce a pleasant sound.) All summer long, he ran up and down the chords and scales. For the first time, he began to hear the relationship between the two. His utter dedication to mastering his instrument set the tone for his stunning fluency soon to come.

Back in Kansas City, Parker practiced for a while with saxophonist Buster Smith and pianist Jay McShann at the Reno club. He then joined Jay McShann's band for a three-week gig at a club called Martin's to finish out the year. With McShann, writes Sadie Cook, he "started to make a name for himself as a hard-swinging taker-of-liberties with jazz harmony."[4] At year's end, Buster Smith went east to try his luck in the Big Apple—New York City.

Beginning in 1937, Charlie Parker (third from left) played off and on with the Jay McShann (seated) Kansas City Orchestra for three and a half years. He left McShann for the last time in 1943 to play with the Earl Hines Band.

On January 10, 1938, Rebecca presented Charlie with a son, Francis Leon Parker. Becoming a father did little to keep Parker at home with his wife. She had little inclination toward her mate's clamorous nightlife. He soon hocked his imported Selmer alto saxophone—bought with insurance money from his auto accident—and hopped a freight train to Chicago. Hocking instruments was to become a signature characteristic with him.

In Chicago, Parker visited the 65 Club where trumpeter King Kolax's band was playing. Band members included singer Billy Eckstine and saxophonist Budd Johnson. Borrowing Andrew "Goon" Gardner's alto sax, Parker sat in and dazzled the seasoned musicians with an extraordinary display of musical prowess. "I guess Bird was no more than about eighteen then," Eckstine recalled later, "but playing like you never heard—wailing alto then."[5] Goon Gardner befriended Parker, lent him a clarinet, and got him a few gigs. But Parker soon tired of Chicago. In characteristic fashion, he hocked Gardner's clarinet and caught a bus to New York City.

In the Big Apple, Parker continued to push the musical envelope. He shunned moderate tempos, preferring to attack the challenging chord changes of upbeat pieces such as "Get Happy" and his personal showpiece, "Cherokee." One night in December 1939, while he was jamming at Dan Wall's Chili House at 7th Avenue and 139th Street, he experienced an artistic epiphany:

Selmer alto saxophone

Now I'd been getting bored with the stereotyped changes that were being used at the time, and I kept thinking there's bound to be something else. I could hear it sometimes but I couldn't play it. Well, that night I was working over "Cherokee," and as I did I found that by using the higher intervals [pitches] of a chord as a melody line and backing them with appropriate [key] changes, I could play the thing I'd been hearing. I came alive.[6]

By playing the top notes of the chords instead of the middle or lower notes (the usual melody notes), he could arrive at a new (melody) line. He tried it, and it worked. No one knew where he was getting the new line; no one in jazz had ever done it before. Parker's breakthrough was his alone, and it set him apart from every other jazz musician.

At the end of 1939, Parker returned home for his father's funeral. Back in Kansas City, he rejoined Jay McShann's band. He remained with McShann off and on for the next three and a half years. "Parker," noted biographer Gary Giddins, "was achieving the kind of fluency that only the greats can claim: complete authority from the first lick [musical phrase], and the ability to sustain the initial inspiration throughout a solo, so that it has dramatic coherence."[7]

While with McShann, Parker —now known to his friends as Yardbird or simply Bird because of his fondness for chicken—made his first recordings. They included "Sepian Bounce," "Jumpin' Blues," and "Lonely Boy Blues." His early records brought him to the attention of a wider jazz audience. Parker's emerging reputation as a harmonic innovator began to spread.

Meanwhile, Rebecca had become pregnant again. Complications set in, however, and she miscarried in July 1940. Later that year, Charlie asked her for a divorce, saying, "If I were free, I think I could become a great musician."[8] She granted his request, and the marriage ended. In January 1942, Jay McShann's itinerant orchestra arrived in New York City for a gig at the Savoy Ballroom. And Charlie Parker—ready now— began his bid for greatness.

Bird in Flight

Charlie Parker drew his musical talents from a spectrum of diverse interests. He admired the classical sophistication of composers Hindesmith and Stravinsky. And he grew up immersed in the primitive directness of the Kansas City blues tradition. He conceived his own sound from the works of altoist Buster Smith and tenor saxophonist Lester Young. "I was crazy about Lester," Parker said, "he played so clean and beautifully."[9]

Lester Young was the leading tenor sax player of his time. Parker transcribed and memorized much of Young's recorded works with the Count Basie Band. He then proceeded to completely overhaul Lester's harmonic and rhythmic concepts, until he had something new to offer. "He was twice as fast as Lester Young and into harmony Lester hadn't touched," recalled jazz drummer Kenny Clarke. "Bird was running the same way we were, but he was way out ahead of us."[10] He was always creating new ideas or concepts—new musical phrases or their development.

Parker put a new twist to the phrase "heart and soul." He put everything into his music. Even his nickname added to the mystique and primal energies of his musical explorations. "*Yardbird* was homely, if not demeaning," observed Ross Russell. "Shortened to *Bird,* it suggested airy flight, light, limitless horizons, otherworldliness."[11] Such was the music of Charlie Parker. No bird ever flew higher or sang sweeter than the Bird from Kansas City.

NAXOS JAZZ LEGENDS

CHARLIE PARKER
Vol.2

BIRD ON THE SIDE

Original Recordings 1941-1947

Highs and Lows

America's entry into World War II overshadowed the debut of McShann's band in Harlem's Savoy Ballroom. Eligible males would soon be required to register for the draft. In Parker's case, evidence of his drug addiction (needle marks) would later exempt him from military service. On opening night, the band shared the stand with the Lucky Millinder Orchestra. Its talented members included trumpeter John Birks "Dizzy" Gillespie.

McShann's rendition of "Clap Hands, Here Comes Charlie" featured Parker on a "walk-on-playing" solo. Parker also starred on a lightning-fast version of "Cherokee." His performance caught the ear of jazz critic Barry Ulanov, who covered the event for *Metronome* magazine: "The jazz set forth by Parker on alto is superb. . . . [He] has a tendency to play too many notes, but his continual search for wild ideas, and the consistency with which he finds them compensates for the weakness that should easily be overcome."[1] Fellow jazzmen also began to talk about a new alto sax man who was years ahead of anyone else.

When Parker was not playing with McShann, he was sitting in at Harlem jam sessions at Monroe's and Minton's Playhouse. (Harlem begins at 110th Street and extends north to 155th Street in New York City.) Familiar faces at such sessions included those of trumpeter Dizzy Gillespie, pianists Thelonious Monk and Bud Powell, guitarist Charlie

Four of Charlie Parker's brothers in jazz shown on front of Minton's Playhouse on 118th Street in Harlem: Thelonious Monk, pianist and composer, Howard McGhee, avant garde trumpeter, Roy Eldridge, swing trumpeter, and Teddy Hill, saxophonist, composer, arranger, and manager of Minton's.

Christian, and drummers Max Roach and Kenny Clarke. Out of their wild improvisations emerged a new kind of jazz called bebop.

Bebop, or bop, is characterized by harmonic complexity, convoluted melodic lines, and constant shifting of accent. It is often played at very rapid tempos. In most accounts, Parker and Gillespie share credit for its creation and advance. Gillespie, however, left no doubt as to bebop's

Charlie Parker
and Dizzy
Gillespie

driving force. "Charlie Parker was the architect of the new sound," Gillespie said later. "He knew how to get from one note to another, the style of the thing. Most of what I did was in the area of harmony and rhythm."[2]

Parker's last recording session with McShann's band came in the summer of 1942. Parker executed a classic opening phrase in "The Jumpin' Blues" that he derived from the recordings of Lester Young. Benny Harris, Earl Hines's trumpeter, later turned it into the theme "Ornithology." Gillespie also incorporated Parker's saxophone riffs (repetitive phrases) in his arrangement of "Disorder at the Border" for Coleman Hawkins.

Right after the session, McShann took his orchestra back to Kansas City on tour. Parker chose to remain among the jazzmen at the forefront of the new sound. "That was the kind of music that caused me to quit McShann and stay in New York,"[3] he said later. Actually, McShann fired him over his increasing unreliability stemming from his drug habit.

For the next few months, Parker picked up occasional gigs along New York's 52nd Street, a strip famous for its array of nightclubs featuring jazz. In December 1942, he hired on as a tenor sax player with Earl "Fatha" Hines's band. The band included Billy Eckstine, Benny Harris, Dizzy Gillespie, vocalist Sarah Vaughn, and other jazz notables.

In April 1943, while touring with Hines in Washington, D.C., Parker met and married dancer Geraldine Marguerite Scott. "When I met him, all he had was a horn and a habit," she recalled later. "He gave me the habit."[4] Geraldine eventually died as a drug addict. Charlie's tenure with Hines lasted only eight months. Hines fired him due to his continuing erratic behavior while on drugs.

Parker joined Billy Eckstine's newly formed band in 1944, sharing the bandstand with Gillespie, Vaughn, and other former members of the Hines band. He left after a few months to play again on 52nd Street with Gillespie, Ben Webster, and others. In February 1945, he joined Gillespie to record on the Guild label. Their notable recordings included "Groovin' High" and "Dizzy Atmosphere," and later "Salt Peanuts," "Shaw Nuff," "Hot House," and "Lover Man" with Vaughn.

Jazz pianist and bandleader Earl "Fatha" Hines (seated) profoundly influenced the development of jazz piano with his amazing technical command and tireless energy. He is shown here with Pvt. Charles Carpenter, former manager of the Hines orchestra.

In the fall of 1945, Parker debuted on the Savoy label. Calling themselves "Charlie Parker's Reboppers," Parker, Gillespie, Miles Davis, bassist Curly Russell, and drummer Max Roach recorded the classics "Ko Ko" and "Now's the Time." Gary Giddins later commented, " 'Ko Ko' was the seminal point of departure for jazz in the postwar era. Its effect paralleled that of [Louis] Armstrong's 'West End Blues' in 1928."[5]

While working the clubs along 52nd Street, Parker had alternating relationships between two women who would play important roles in his remaining years—Doris Sydnor and Chan Richardson. They were complete opposites. Doris was a painfully thin mothering type; Chan, a vivacious dancer and ex-model. Parker probably welcomed the opportunity to get away from his complicated love affairs for a while. He agreed to play a gig with Gillespie at Billy Berg's club in Hollywood in December 1945.

While in Hollywood, Parker and Gillespie recorded several sessions on Ross Russell's Dial Records label. Gillespie returned to New York, but Parker remained in Los Angeles and continued to record for Dial. These sessions produced a treasury of some of Parker's best work, including "Yardbird Suite," "Max the Mooche," and

"A Night in Tunisia." Despite Parker's superlative work on Dial, his personal life was spinning out of control.

On July 29, 1946, while in the throes of drug withdrawal, Parker fell asleep with a lighted cigarette and set fire to his hotel room. Local authorities later charged him with indecent exposure (for wandering about the hotel lobby wearing only his socks), resisting arrest, and suspected arson. Parker's high life abruptly plunged to an unintended low. He served the next six months as an unwilling guest at the Camarillo State (mental) Hospital.

Best of Bird

In Charlie Parker's approach to musical composition, he often inserted original melodies, or "lines," over preexisting jazz standards or forms. Though this method predated bebop, progressive jazz musicians made it a signature of their movement. Jazz artists gradually moved away from arranging popular standards and began to compose their own material. The following titles provide a representative sampling of Parker's body of work—or, as some might say, the best of Bird:

"Billie's Bounce," named for agent Billy Shaw's secretary, is one of Parker's few blues compositions. Its short saxophone solo showcases his ability to tailor his playing to the demands of any situation.

"Ornithology" derives its theme from a phrase that Parker first improvised over Jay McShann's "The Jumpin' Blues." It originally came from a composition crafted by Benny Harris over the standard "How High the Moon."

"Yardbird Suite"—based on "What Price Love?"—bears Parker's nickname. It features his agility and concise phrasing over chord changes. He demonstrates his knowledge and mastery of the 32-bar song.

In "Now's the Time," Parker performs the blues over six choruses. His use of repetitions conveys his deep perception of and connection to the elemental blues form.

"Anthropology," also known as "Thriving from a Riff," features Parker's daring performance at breakneck tempo of his original line over the chord progression of "I Got Rhythm." Many of today's jazzmen still include these rhythm changes in their repertoire.

Chapter **5**

Flying
Home

Parker rested for six months at Camarillo State Hospital, ate a lot, and put on about sixty pounds. Doris Sydnor came out from New York and worked as a waitress to be near him. He was released from the hospital in January 1947 in pretty good health. In February, he joined pianist Errol Garner, trumpeter Howard McGhee, tenor player Wardell Gray, and others in more recording sessions for Ross Russell's Dial label. "Ornithology" and "Relaxin' at Camarillo" came out of these sessions. After the final session, Parker packed his horn and said, "That's all she wrote. When I lay my head down next it's going to be in the [Big] Apple."[1] He returned to New York in April that year.

In December, Parker left on a cross-country tour with promoter Norman Granz's Jazz at the Philharmonic. After his return to New York in 1948, he led a quintet for a while, at various times featuring trumpeter Miles Davis, pianists Duke Jordan and Al Haig, and drummer Max Roach. They played such clubs as Royal Roost, Three Deuces, Bop City, and others.

In September, Parker cut "Parker's Mood" for Savoy Records. It is acclaimed as one of Parker's finest blues numbers. Jazz writer Brian Priestley noted, "The alto digs down to the roots of black music while majestically updating its language."[2] At year's end, while on the West Coast, Parker and Sydnor slipped off to Tijuana, Mexico, and tied the knot. Whether he first bothered to divorce Geraldine remains unclear.

Charlie Parker, producer Ross Russell, drummer Harold "Doc" West, singer Earl Coleman, who sang like Billy Ekstine, and bassist, trumpeter, and composer John Willie "Shifty" Henry at a Dial recording session of "Dark Shadows" in Hollywood, February 1947.

Parker closed out 1948 and began 1949 recording with Machito's Afro-Cuban orchestra on the Verve label. Billed as "Charlie Parker Plays South of the Border," the session featured two long Parker solos, "No Noise" and "Mango Manque." In May, traveling to Europe for the first time, Parker played the International Jazz Festival in Paris.

Later that year, in November, Parker debuted with a string section. *Charlie Parker with Strings,* recorded under the Mercury label, produced several sides. "Just Friends" stood out from the rest. "The alto saxophone soars majestically over the lush background," remarked Ross Russell. "Its tone is brilliant and its virtuosity compelling."[3] The following month, Birdland, a new club named for Parker, opened on Harlem's 52nd Street.

Parker played at Birdland a lot in 1950. Early in the year, Doris began to tire of trying to keep his life and finances in order. She eventually went home to her mother. "I was in no physical condition to cope with the erratic life of a jazz musician," she explained later, adding, "I just couldn't take the anxiety of wondering where he was the nights he came home very late or not at all."[4]

In July, Parker entered into a common-law marriage with ex-dancer and model Chan Richardson. She bore him two children: a girl, Pree; and a boy, Laird Baird. (Pree died at age three of a congenital heart condition.) Charlie capped off the year with another tour abroad, this

A recording session of *Charlie Parker with Strings,* featuring (from left to right) drummer Buddy Rich, bassist Ray Brown, saxophonist Charlie Parker, conductor Mitch Miller, violinist Max Hollander, possibly arranger Jimmy Carroll, and violinist Milton Lomask.

time to Sweden, France, and England. Back in the United States, he suffered a severe attack from a peptic ulcer, but he recovered after hospitalization.

In 1951, New York's Alcoholic Beverage Control Board rescinded Parker's cabaret card for nearly two years for a drug-related reason. Without the card, he could not work in any club within the state that served liquor. As a result, his agent Billy Shaw sent him on gigs out of state.

Parker opened at the Tiffany Club in Los Angeles in May 1952, then moved on to a gig at San Francisco's Say When club. He returned to New York in September to play a benefit dance in Harlem's Rockland Palace. A dynamic up-tempo version of Lester Young's "Lester Leaps In" highlighted the brilliance of Parker's performance. During the following year, 1953, his life and career slipped into a dizzying downward plunge.

Parker continued to suffer from bleeding ulcers. He tried to ease the pain with more drugs and alcohol. Gigs became infrequent because of various job disputes he had taken to union arbitration. His first wife, Rebecca, sued him for unpaid child support. His common-law wife, Chan, left him. Torn by exhaustion and depression, Parker began to come apart. "That he could summon forth strength and radiance until nearly the end is borne out by tapes that document his playing through the end of 1954," wrote Gary Giddins. "But there were other nights when admirers turned away in embarrassment."[5]

Ironically, on Saturday, March 5, 1955, Charlie "the Bird" Parker played his last gig at Birdland, the jazz club named for him.

The apartment on Fifth Avenue was silent except for Parker's protests. "That's out!" he tells Dr. Freymann. "I'm not going to any hospital!"[6] His tone left no room for discussion. The doctor knew he could not force Parker to go to the hospital against his will. Nica, with her daughter, volunteered to care for Parker around the clock in her apartment.

Dr. Freymann reluctantly consented to Nica's proposal. "I have to warn you that this man may die at any moment," he cautioned. "He has

Four of the all-time greats of jazz onstage at Birdland, the famous jazz night spot named after Charlie Parker's nickname, "Yardbird" or simply "Bird." From left to right, Tommy Porter on bass, Charlie Parker on alto saxophone, Dizzy Gillespie on trumpet, and John Coltrane on tenor saxophone.

advanced cirrhosis and stomach ulcers. He must not leave here except in an ambulance."[7]

Three days passed. By Saturday, March 12, 1955, Parker felt better. Propped up in an easy chair with pillows and blankets, he sat watching the Tommy Dorsey program on television. Suddenly, he rose from the chair and choked once or twice, then dropped back into the chair, unconscious. The baroness rushed over to him and felt his pulse. She felt a weak throb at first, then nothing.

"I didn't want to believe it," she would say later. "But I really knew that Bird was dead."[8] At the moment of his passing, a great clap of thunder rattled the apartment. It was 8:45 P.M. The Bird was on the wing—flying home.

Whatever else Charlie Parker may have been, he was first and foremost a musical genius. Musicians searching for something new and different would sell their souls to sit in with Parker and get the "word from the Bird."[9]

Parker created a legion of followers on the saxophone. His influence was not limited to that instrument, however. He affected how every other musical instrument was played. His tone and technique, combined with his concepts of harmony and melody, lifted jazz to a whole new level. "Only Louis Armstrong in the 1920s had caused such a tidal change in the way the music was played,"[10] scribed jazz writer Brian Priestley.

Dr. Robert Freymann did not know Parker's age at the time of his passing. Based on his appearance and physical condition, Freymann estimated his age at fifty-three. Parker died at age thirty-four. He had lived his entire life up-tempo. His mind and body reflected the enormous ravages of high times and self-abuse.

"No one had such a love of life," jazz impresario Robert Reisner wrote of Parker, "and no one tried harder to kill himself."[11] When the music stops, it's time to pay the music-makers. Parker's wages came in the form of death before his time—and a world enriched by the music he left behind.

"Music is your own experience, your thoughts, your wisdom," Parker said. "If you don't live it, it won't come out your horn. They teach you there's a boundary line to music. But, man, there's no boundary line to art."[12] Parker knew a lot about life and art.

• DATES • PERSONNEL DETAILS • NOTES

CHARLIE PARKER
A Studio Chronicle
1940 - 1948

5 CDs
REMASTERED
125 SIDES

RECORDINGS THAT ARE AMONG THE MOST IMPORTANT EVER MADE

1920	Charles Christopher Parker Jr. Is born to Charles and Addie Parker in Kansas City, Kansas, on August 29.
1927	Charlie and his parents move to Kansas City, Missouri. His father leaves soon after and Charlie's mother is left to raise him on her own.
1931	Charlie's mother buys him a saxophone and he begins taking lessons.
1935	Charlie goes to Lincoln High School. He drops out soon after to pursue music full-time.
1936	He marries Rebecca Ruffin at the age of 16.
1938	Parker's first son, Francis Leon Parker, is born.
1939	Parker visits New York City for the first time. He plays with local jazz bands for about a year and it greatly influences his music style.
1940	Parker first joined McShann for a three-week gig in 1937; he later rejoined McShann as a permanent member of the band in 1940 and played off and on with him for three and a half years.
1943	Parker marries Geraldine Scott.
1945	Parker and his friend Dizzy Gillespie start recording the first bop songs. They go on a Hollywood tour together in Los Angeles, California.
1946	Parker suffers a mental breakdown due to a combination of drug addiction and stress caused by criticism of his music by older, more-established musicians. He spends six months recovering in a state hospital.
1947–1951	Parker performs in nightclubs, radio stations, and other venues as a soloist and with other musicians. He travels to Paris, France, and Scandinavia on tour with Norman Granz's "Jazz at the Harmonic."
1948	Parker marries Doris Snydor.
1949	The nightclub "Birdland" is opened in New York in Parker's honor.
1950	He marries Chan Richardson.
1954	As his health declines and debt piles up, Parker attempts suicide twice. He willingly commits himself to Bellevue Hospital in New York.
1955	He makes his last public appearance at Birdland on March 5. Parker dies of heart failure, pneumonia, and cirrhosis of the liver eight days later.

Discography

1977 Charlie Parker: The Verve Years (1952–54), Verve
1988 Charlie Parker at Storyville, Blue Note (recorded 1953)
1989 Charlie Parker: The Legendary Dial Masters Vol.I, Stash
1991 Charlie Parker: "Round Midnight and Other Gems," Tel-Star
1992 Bird at St. Nick's, Original Jazz Classics (recorded 1950)
1993 Charlie Parker: Jazz at the Philharmonic 1949, Verve
1994 Bird on 52nd Street, Original Jazz Classics (recorded 1948)
Charlie Parker Plays Standards, Jazz Masters 28, Verve
1995 Charlie Parker: South of the Border (recorded 1951–52)
1996 Charlie Parker: The Complete Dial Recordings, Rhino
1997 Bird and Diz (recorded 1948) Verve
Yardbird Suite: The Ultimate Charlie Parker, Rhino

Chapter 1   Changing Directions

1. Robert George Reisner, *Bird: The Legend of Charlie Parker* (New York: Citadel Press, 1965), p. 14.
2. Ross Russell, *Bird Lives: The High Life and Hard Times of Charlie (Yardbird) Parker* (London: Quartet Books, 1972), p. 349.
3. Ibid.
4. Ibid.
5. Ibid.
6. Ibid.
7. Ibid., p. 351.
8. Ibid.

Chapter 2   Fast Company

1. Gary Giddins, *Celebrating Bird: The Triumph of Charlie Parker* (New York: Beech Tree Books, 1987), p. 38.
2. Ibid., p. 39.
3. Ibid., p. 40.
4. Ross Russell, *Bird Lives: The High Life and Hard Times of Charlie (Yardbird) Parker* (London: Quartet Books, 1972), p. 84.
5. Ibid., p. 85.
6. Ibid.
7. Ibid., p. 66.

Chapter 3   Ready Now

1. Ross Russell, *Bird Lives: The High Life and Hard Times of Charlie (Yardbird) Parker* (London: Quartet Books, 1972), p. 74.
2. Brian Priestley, *Chasin' the Bird: The Life and Legacy of Charlie Parker* (New York: Oxford University Press, 2005), p. 20.
3. Ibid.
4. Sadie Cook, ed., *In Session with Charlie Parker* (London: International Music Publications, 1999), p. 4.
5. Robert George Reisner, *Bird: The Legend of Charlie Parker* (New York: Citadel Press, 1965), p. 84.
6. Gary Giddins, *Celebrating Bird: The Triumph of Charlie Parker* (New York: Beech Tree Books, 1987), p. 56.

7. Ibid., pp. 60–61.
8. Ken Vail, *Bird's Diary* (Chessington, Surrey UK: Castle Communications, 1996). p. 5.
9. Cook, p. 6.
10. Russell, p. 138.
11. Ibid., p. 181.

Chapter 4   Highs and Lows

1. Ross Russell, *Bird Lives: The High Life and Hard Times of Charlie (Yardbird) Parker* (London: Quartet Books, 1972), p. 126.
2. Gary Giddins, *Celebrating Bird: The Triumph of Charlie Parker* (New York: Beech Tree Books, 1987), p. 68.
3. Brian Priestley, *Chasin' the Bird: The Life and Legacy of Charlie Parker* (New York: Oxford University Press, 2005), p. 34.
4. Giddins, p. 71.
5. Ibid., p. 88.

Chapter 5   Flying Home

1. Ross Russell, *Bird Lives: The High Life and Hard Times of Charlie (Yardbird) Parker* (London: Quartet Books, 1972), p. 240.
2. Brian Priestley, *Chasin' the Bird: The Life and Legacy of Charlie Parker* (New York: Oxford University Press, 2005), p. 64.
3. Russell, p. 273.
4. Priestley, p. 81.
5. Gary Giddins, *Celebrating Bird: The Triumph of Charlie Parker* (New York: Beech Tree Books, 1987), p. 115.
6. Russell, p. 352.
7. Ibid., p. 353.
8. Ken Vail, *Bird's Diary* (Chessington, Surrey UK: Castle Communications, 1996). p. 174.
9. Priestley, p. 57.
10. Ibid.
11. Robert George Reisner, *Bird: The Legend of Charlie Parker* (New York: Citadel Press, 1965), p. 15
12. Ibid., p. 27.

BOOKS

Brown, Jeremy K. *Stevie Wonder.* New York: Infobase Publishing/Chelsea House, 2010.

Ford, Carin T. *Duke Ellington: "I Live With Music".* Berkeley Heights, New Jersey: Enslow Publishers, 2007.

Llanas, Sheila Griffin. *Hip-Hop Stars.* Mankato, Minnesota: Capstone Press, 2010.

Lynette, Rachel. *Miles Davis: Legendary Jazz Musician.* Farmington Hills, Michigan: KidHaven Press, 2010.

Partridge, Kenneth. *Louis Armstrong.* New York: Infobase Publishing/Chelsea House, 2011.

WORKS CONSULTED

Cook, Sadie, ed. *In Session with Charlie Parker.* London: International Music Publications, 1999.

Giddins, Gary. *Celebrating Bird: The Triumph of Charlie Parker.* New York: Beech Tree Books, 1987.

Gold, Robert S. *A Jazz Lexicon.* New York: Alfred A. Knopf, 1964.

Gray, James Martin. *Blues for Bird.* Victoria, British Columbia: Ekstasis Editions Canada, 1993.

Priestley, Brian. *Chasin' the Bird: The Life and Legacy of Charlie Parker.* New York: Oxford University Press, 2005.

Reisner, Robert George. *Bird: The Legend of Charlie Parker.* New York: Citadel Press, 1965.

Russell, Ross. *Bird Lives: The High Life and Hard Times of Charlie (Yardbird) Parker.* London: Quartet Books, 1972.

Vail, Ken. *Bird's Diary.* Chessington, Surrey, UK: Castle Communications, 1996.

ON THE INTERNET

All Music: Scott Yanow, *Charlie Parker: Biography*
    http://allmusic.com/artist/charlie-parker-p112401/biography
Charlie Parker Online
    http://www.john-coltrane.com/charlie-bird-parker.htm
Jazz Institute of Chicago: Stuart Nicholson, *Charlie Parker*
    http://www.jazzinchicago.org/educates/journal/reviews/charlie-parker

ON THE INTERNET

JazzStuff: Biographies: Lauren Peterson, *Charlie Parker*
   http://www.jazzine.com/jazzstuff/biographies/charlie_parker.phtml
The Official Site of Charlie "Yardbird" Parker—Biography
   http://www.cmgww.com/music/parker/about/biography.html

PHOTO CREDITS: Cover—Joe Rasemas; pp. 4, 18, 32—William Gottlieb/Redferns/Getty Images; pp. 6, 8, 16, 34, 35, 36—cc-by-sa; p. 9—Barbara Marvis; pp. 10, 12—Michael Ochs Archives/Getty Images; p. 13—Gjon Mili/Time Life Pictures/Getty Images; p. 15—Herb Snitzer/Michael Ochs Archives/Getty Images; pp. 20, 38—Frank Diggs Collection/Getty Images; p. 24—Bob Parent/Getty Images; p. 26—Library of Congress; p. 27—Herman Leonard; p. 29—National Archives; Every effort has been made to locate all copyright holders of material used in this book. If any errors or omissions have occurred, corrections will be made in future editions of the book.

BIRD LIVES

bar (bahr)—One of the vertical lines dividing a piece of music into equal units.

beat (beet)—A recurring emphasis marking rhythm in music or poetry.

bebop (BEE-bohp)—Bop; jazz characterized by harmonic complexity, convoluted melodic lines, and constant shifting of accent and often played at very rapid tempos.

blues (blooz)—Melancholy jazz melodies originating from African American rhythms and lyrics.

chord (kord)—A combination of notes sounded together in harmony.

harmony (HAHR-moh-nee)—A pleasant chord or progression of chords.

harmonic (hahr-MON-ik)—An overtone of a primary note played on an instrument.

improvise (IM-proh-vihz)—To compose, recite, play, or sing on the spur of the moment; **improvisation** (im-proh-vih-ZAY-shun)—The act of improvising.

jazz (jaz)—Music of American origin characterized by improvisation, syncopation, and usually a regular or forceful rhythm.

key (kee)—A system of related notes based on a particular note; the tone or pitch of a voice.

melody (MEL-oh-dee)—A sweet or agreeable arrangement or succession of sounds; a rhythmic succession of single tones organized as a pleasurable whole.

music (MYOO-zik)—Vocal, instrumental, or mechanical sounds having rhythm, melody, or harmony.

note (noht)—A tone; a written symbol used to indicate duration and pitch of a tone by its shape and position on the staff.

pitch (pich)—The degree of highness or lowness of a musical note or a voice.

rhythm (RITH-em)—An ordered recurrent alternation of strong and weak elements in the flow of sound; the pattern produced by the emphasis and duration of notes in music.

scale (skayl)—An arrangement of notes in a musical system, ascending and descending by fixed intervals.

swing (swing)—A kind of jazz that varies the time of the melody while keeping the accompaniment in strict time.

syncopation (sing-koh-PAY-shohn)—A change to the accents in a passage of music caused typically by stressing the weak beat rather than the strong one (or vice versa).

tempo (TEM-poh)—The time or speed or rhythm of a piece of music.

tone (tohn)—A musical or vocal sound, especially with reference to its pitch and quality and strength.

triumvirate (try-UM-vuh-rit)—A powerful allegiance of three strong people.

About the Author

Earle Rice Jr. is a former senior design engineer and technical writer in the aerospace, electronic-defense, and nuclear industries. He has devoted full time to his writing since 1993 and is the author of more than sixty published books. A lifelong jazz buff, he grew up listening to the bluesy tenor of his musician father's saxophone. Rice is listed in *Who's Who in America* and is a member of the Society of Children's Book Writers and Illustrators, the League of World War I Aviation Historians, the Air Force Association, and the Disabled American Veterans.